Celebrating the Woman You Are

S. Suzanne Mayer, IHM

Paulist Press
New York/Mahwah, New Jersey

The publisher gratefully acknowledges use of the following: Excerpt from "Live," LIVE OR DIE by Anne Sexton. Copyright © 1966 by Anne Sexton. Reprinted by permission of Houghton Mifflin Co. All rights reserved. Excerpt from SELECTED POETRY OF JESSICA POWERS edited by Regina Siegfried and Robert Morneau. Reprinted by permission of Sheed & Ward.

Cover/book design and interior illustrations by Nicholas T. Markell.

Library of Congress Cataloging-in-Publication Data

Mayer, S. Suzanne, 1946-
     Celebrating the woman you are / by S. Suzanne Mayer.
          p.   cm.
     Includes bibliographical references.
     ISBN 0-8091-3559-0
     1. Women—Religious life. 2. Mayer, S. Suzanne, 1946- 3. Spiritual life—Christianity. I. Title.
BV4527.M34   1995
248.8´43—dc20   94-49164
                                                                                    CIP

Published by Paulist Press
997 Macarthur Boulevard
Mahwah, New Jersey 07430

Printed and bound in the
United States of America

Contents

Dedication

For my sisters—
those in my family
and those in my community
for the women they are
and the women they have called me to become

IlluminationBooks
A Foreword

*I*lluminationBooks bring to light wonderful ideas, helpful information, and sound spirituality in concise, illustrative, readable, and eminently practical works on topics of current concern. Learning from stress; interior peace; personal prayer; biblical awareness; walking with others in darkness; appreciating the love already in our lives; spiritual discernment; uncovering helpful psychological antidotes for our tendency to worry too much at times; and important guides to improving interpersonal relations, are only several of the areas which will be covered in this series.

The goal of each IlluminationBook, then, is to provide great ideas, helpful steps, and needed inspiration in small volumes. Each book offers a new beginning for the reader to explore possibilities and embrace practicalities which can be employed in everyday life.

In today's busy and anxious world, Illumination-Books are meant to provide a source of support—without requiring an inordinate amount of time or prior preparation. Each small work stands on its own. Hopefully, the information provided not only will be nourishing in itself but also will encourage further exploration in the area.

One is obviously never done learning. With every morsel of wisdom each of these books provides, the goal is to keep the process of seeking knowledge ongoing even during busy times, when sitting down with a larger work is impossible or undesirable.

However, more than information (as valuable as it is), at the base of each work in the series is a deep sense of *hope* that is based on a belief in the beautiful statement made by Jesus to his disciples and in turn to us: "You are my friends" (Jn 15:15).

As "friends of God" we must seek the presence of the Lord in ourselves, in others, in silence and solitude, in nature, and in daily situations. IlluminationBooks are designed to provide implicit and explicit opportunities to appreciate this reality in new ways. So, it is in this spirit that this book and the other ones in the series are offered to you.
                                                    —*Robert J. Wicks*
                                General Editor, IlluminationBooks

Introduction

*T*he other day as I crossed the autumn fields near home, my eyes were drawn to the skies by the raucous honking of the Canadian geese who have made our corner of the world part of their migratory pattern. Against the deep blue of a fall morning, the sharp black V-pattern was etched. It reminded me of that lovely story written by Paul Gallico in which he recounts as a modern allegory the comings and goings of another migratory bird, The Snow Goose.

The story is a simple one of a wounded bird found far from home on the southern coast of England by a small gypsy-spirited girl and nursed back to health and flight by the solitary inhabitant of an abandoned lighthouse who has built a refuge for the wildfowl among the marshes of the area. Interestingly, as I remembered the story, read some twenty years ago, it struck me as eminently masculine. I recalled the closing events in particular—the heat and fire of Dunkirk, the almost epic figure of the lone boatman plowing the war-ravaged waters, the incidents of courage under fire, the sense of comradeship in the telling and retelling.

My memory of it impelled me to take it up again. After haunting bookstores and library shelves I found an old, obviously little used copy. Most remarkably, the story I read in this present moment was distinctly different in its tone, its theme, even in its characters from that one recalled some two decades past. The three central figures remain, of course, the nucleus around which the few incidents revolve. Rhayader still looms from the mists of his isolated refuge, an almost gargoyle creature of twisted body and indomitable spirit. At the end he still performs the feats of heroism for which his legend is sung. But from the first page he also portrays an *anima*, a gentle nurturing presence, the soul of the artistic, sensitive person who longs for love and human compassion and companionship.

Firth still dances through his life, a gamin spirit, untamed as the wild birds that flock to the refuge. However, this time she also emerges as a young woman moving toward adulthood with a thirst for an identity forged through intimacy. Her fears are those of one not yet willing to risk love. Her triumph is that of the "valiant woman" of Old Testament acclaim, who "reaches out to touch the poor and the needy" (Prov 31:20), who has mastered the gift of maturity—of holding on, then letting go.

Then, finally, there is the huge white bird that hovers like the creative spirit of Genesis above the dynamics of these two persons, above the several incidents of the story, filling a world torn with violence with a sense of peace, a time marked with separation and with the riches of fidelity, commitment and promise. She is classically maternal in that she brings out of the death-throes of loss the birth pangs of newness. She is elusively enigmatic in that the life force she brings is as much one of shadow as light. The mystical *Lost Princess*, as Rhayader names her, stands as an archetype of the feminine and its movement toward growth and toward God.

As I looked at my two readings separated by two decades I wondered what could have inspired the difference. How could a story recalled as so imprinted with the masculine be so alive with the feminine? The story obviously has remained unchanged across the years. In fact, the very copy of the book could well be the same one I read that time past. What has changed is both my world and myself.

From both perspectives, I am reminded of those now classic experiments in visual perception in which the subjects were given inverting lenses to wear for a period of time. At first their world literally turned upside down and

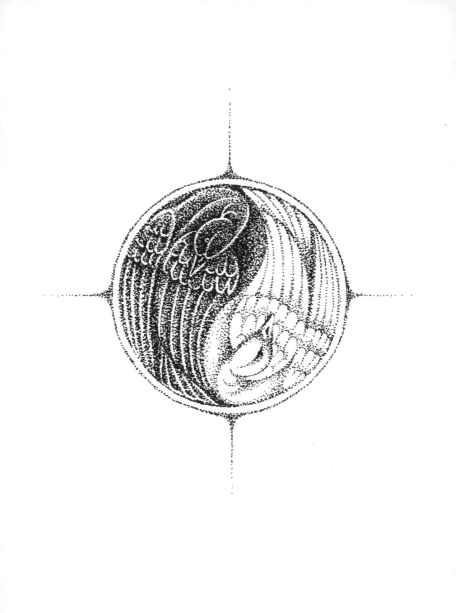

they became both physically and psychologically disoriented. But after a period of adjustment, they learned to cope with a world standing on its head. In fact, they did it so well that when the lenses were removed the subjects needed another time of readjustment to focus on a world upright again.

Over the past few years I have met many women who have companioned me on a search into a world just becoming. Clients I have worked with in therapy, students I have encountered in classes I have taught, mothers and grandmothers of young persons identified as "at risk," and most especially Sisters of my own community and other religious groups working to make transformation real—these have been my fellow journeyers. From their experiences and the challenge to learn in order to help them and meet them in their growth paths, I have been drinking in like a sponge many of the writings, findings and even questions that have arisen in the area of feminine psychology and spirituality.

From the work of researchers like Carol Gilligan, Ruthellen Josselson, Jean Miller and others working along the lines of female development and maturation, I and these women with whom I have been associated have come to look at a world once seemingly fixed in place and view it with new eyes, in many respects set upside down. What had been presented for decades, at times centuries, as normative because of male theorists working out of male models and using male subjects as reference groups, has been placed under the scrutiny of new lenses. We are asking what can we hold on to and what must be made new. What words speak to us of our experience and resonate in our lives as we fashion them and what must be reformed and refashioned for us to hear truth. In particular, the revisioning of feminine development as linked to mutuality, relationship and a whole ethic of care has transformed the understanding of what women bring to their efforts toward self-direction and self-definition.

As our horizons have shifted and we have sought new centers of balance and new directions in terms of our psychosocial and emotional growth, we have looked for new visions in charting our path to God. Voices, long silenced, weakened with disenfranchisement or challenged into submission, have assumed a new power, a resonance. So biblical women have emerged from the shadows of cultural and socio-ethnic exile to share stories of how they found God and even more of how God found them. Biblical themes have been reconsidered and exegesis has been reworked in terms of women's issues and women's insights. Models of prayer and spiritual journeying that evoke feminine forms, that follow female guides and that struggle with feminine hurts have emerged as evocative of God. The shift has taken place so that the value of more feminine approaches to God—approaches that emphasize intuition, affective prayer, mystical union, passionate love, gentleness, compassion and body-awareness—has come to be recognized, not just *by* women, but *because* of them.

And what has happened on the broad horizon of feminine spirituality and psychology has happened in the much more narrow scope of my own life and heart. In myself and in the women who form the community of discourse against which I test and measure my personal insights I have heard new words formulated, new ideas tested, new visions enunciated. They speak of moving toward God through their weaknesses and rejoicing not in the hurt but in the gold wrought in the "refiner's fire." They share stories of tragedy and triumph and in the sharing form new stories. They live with the questions and in the between-time rejoice that they are alive to see, if not the final outcomes, at least the gestation period.

So what happened for me with the beautiful allegory of *The Snow Goose* signifies what has happened and continues to happen for women in a world of growth and spiritual longing. The old is transformed by a new vision and certain images emerge from the shadows. A voice is empowered to speak and truths are uttered.

In this IlluminationBook, I offer not revolutionary ideas but reconsiderations—a few themes that suggest possibilities for reflection, response, revisioning. In treating each of these I follow a simple design: the presentation of the theme as it calls to women in the here and now, a sharing of that theme as it resonates in my life and those of the women whose stories I share and a closing on a focus figure—a contemporary woman who for me images and personifies this theme. The women I have chosen are not saints in either the ecclesial or even conventional meaning of the word. In many cases their inclusion is because of their flaws, for in their moments of grief and failure they stand for me as truly human, truly striving, and therefore truly women.

In all of this I do what the title of this book states—I celebrate woman—the woman I am beginning to realize as possible, the woman who stands on a horizon of possibility. Recently, I attended the jubilee celebration of a Sister who was marking twenty-five years of service as a woman religious. I was deeply touched by her theme of journeying which celebrated both the valleys and peaks of her life during those years. She echoed the words of Joy Lewis, the dying wife of C.S. Lewis so recently captured in film, who she said very simply—"The happiness now is part of the pain then. That's the deal." This book recognizes that double-edged sword that is the celebration of woman now, a sword that "shall pierce to the soul so that the secret truths of many may be bared" (Luke 2:35). It is in this sweet-sour reality that the celebration takes place.

A final note: I celebrate the woman I am, the women I know and in a very real sense, all women. Much of what I say can be said, too, of many men who have entered my life—have taught, supervised, counseled, sacramentalized and most especially fathered and supported me. The feminine comes more naturally to most women and so in celebrating women, I also applaud the men who have taken the harder challenge of incorporating into their lives many of the dynamics which I shall address.

Chapter One
A Woman Celebrates Interiority

*T*o celebrate—*etymologists trace the origins to the Latin and associate it with the root that means "to frequent," as in to visit often. To me celebrate suggests something far more: a party—with people and laughter, food and sharing, closeness and a communal experience that triggers happiness.*

When I meditate on the word celebrate, a scriptural image comes to mind, a vision of feet stamping in the dust, of music playing and many voices raised in joyful song. It's a dance. Only infrequently in the Old Testament does an author record an instance of dancing; yet, for these tribal people, just emerging from a whole culture of

pagan ritual and worship, it would seem that dance would be as much a part of their life as eating or harvesting. One record of such an event occurs in Exodus 15. The Israelites had just experienced the miracle of deliverance, crossing the dry land that had once been the wall-high waters of the Red Sea. Miriam, that enigmatic sister of the deliverers Aaron and Moses, suddenly realizes freedom is theirs. In the joy and triumph of the moment she seizes her tambourine and waving it in the air with a burst of song begins the victory dance. Her exuberance is contagious and suddenly behind her "all the women follow" (vs. 20), playing and singing to the Lord.

In the person of Miriam so much that is woman is represented in this short pericope of scripture. She is open and alive to the moment. It is she and she alone who recognizes freedom at the instant that it becomes her people's birthright. That realization becomes so full in her that she gives birth to it, pouring forth what is within her and spilling it out upon others, transmitting life and calling to God-awareness. Her birthing captures the whole of her, body and spirit, and so her rejoicing takes the form of body-prayer. From the depths of her spirit comes the ecstasy that shows itself in her movement, her song, her very being. Finally, around her forms community, a sisterhood that with her shares her story and in her witness becomes one. So much that is Miriam is woman as she is to be celebrated.

Interesting, that it is the woman Miriam who becomes the leader of this festive moment. In other scriptural passages in which the Hebrews celebrate victory, the leader of the triumphant procession is male. True, in most recorded instances, it is David, the poet, musician and visionary, who seizes the moment and the song. But in the Exodus account the moment is given to Miriam. Why she?

A point that is made subtly, but certainly, occurs in the descriptive title given her as she initiates the dance. She is designated as "the prophetess Miriam." While modern connotations of prophet (or its feminine derivative) suggest a seer, a soothsayer, a fortune teller, more accurately and scripturally, a prophet is one who speaks truth, a truth that comes from an inward call, a truth that communicates to humans the word of God written on the soul of the speaker.

Such is Miriam in her moment of celebration. She grasps deep within her being the import of this moment. Freedom is won. A people is being born. A whole new world is opening up. God had told her brothers in many words with many signs and on many occasions the same truth. They in their own way had transmitted these words to the people frequently during the pre-exodus days. But the reality had somehow been buried with the mud-bricks and fleshpots in Egypt; the words lost on the winds of change that transfixed the people. It was left to this strange, sometimes shortsighted and stubborn woman to sense the whole truth, to catch the trace of the divine as it enters into human history and to give voice and life to it in her dance.

This is the first theme of woman that we celebrate—her gift of touching on truth within, the gift of interiority. Moving from the historical books of early scripture to the prophetic closing book of the New Testament, we find in Revelation a paradoxical and elusive image: "The One who sat on the throne said to me, 'See, I make all things new . . . I am Alpha and Omega, Beginning and End'" (Rev 21:5-6). The omega, the last letter of the Greek alphabet, for centuries has stood for totality. Tied, to the initial alpha in three passages of Revelation (1:8, 21:6, 22:13), it symbolizes a completeness, a movement from beginning to end that subsumes both. Placed in the mouth of the "One who sat on the throne," omega epitomizes a new vision of apocalyptic union, a new creation of fulfillment, possible only with the end time.

Some twenty centuries after the unknown prophet John penned his apocalyptic text, a struggling mid-life poet fashioned her own image of omega. Anne Sexton writes in "Live" from her book of poetry *Live or Die*:

> "Today life opened inside me like an egg
> and there inside
> after considerable digging
> I found the answer."

This twentieth-century woman, known more for her wrestling with themes of agony and loss, celebrates her discovery of the source and purpose of life in contemporary woman's condition, her experience, her coming to identity. Both physically and spiritually, life for Sexton is contained in the sun-yolked egg that happens for her and within her when she enters into the place where life is begotten.

A woman, then, celebrates the gift of interiority by coming to a sense of her inwardness, first in a bodily sense and then in a transcendental sense that speaks to her of union with God. In the physical sense, the concept of inner space has been explored in recent years by both researchers and therapists with definite ramifications for women. Some of the most powerful insights come from those treating women marked by a devastating lack of inner space. I have met such women and heard their stories. These women struggle with terrible experiences of emptiness, of utter depletion and hopelessness. Often victims of severe early trauma, of mother-absence who wrestle with problems of body image, they speak of themselves as "empty vessels," as "ciphers." One woman told me whenever she heard the gospel words to the pharisees about being "whitewashed tombs full of dead man's bones" (Matt 23:27), she thought of herself and her life. Their self-definitions evoke images of T.S. Eliot's "hollow men," sterile "wind in dry grass." One therapist, analyzing the drawings done by one young woman lacking inner space, notes the repetition of closed circles, locked spheres that permit no entry, that remain empty. When her patient moved to healing and a sense of inner space, the images changed. They became open ovals, semicircles, in one case, the tracing of a baby resting in its mother's arms—the omega. Paradoxically, what these clients speak of in this experience of new-found inner space is not a movement to fullness but rather to a "positive emptiness," not filled space but potential space.

On a spiritual, metaphorical level, the omega speaks of the gift a woman holds for exploring the space within. Analogously, women are religious cave explorers, climbing down into the depths to discover whole worlds. I remember the first time I toured the crystal cathedral chambers of one of the many caverns in my native Pennsylvania. Around me loomed the huge rock structures that so resembled the marble halls of medieval churches. What struck me was that a few minutes before, when I had been walking around on the surface, I had gone along blissfully unaware that this whole world of wonder and beauty lay literally underneath my feet. As women enter into the gift of interiority, they become spiritual spelunkers. The worlds they enter are not new creations; they have lain within since conception—potential emptiness—awaiting their arrival. In order to come to know their secrets, to realize the beauty locked in the dark, the woman must spiral down to her depths. The modern mystic Thomas Merton came to this realization during his years of searching, centering and entering in. He noted that when the "I awakens, the person finds within the Presence of Him Whose image he is. And, by a paradox beyond all human expression, God and the soul seem to have but one single I."

If this all seems more the experience of the mystic

than the ordinary woman, in a way it is and in a truer way it is not. The mystic is, after all, one who, with Catherine of Genoa, that recognized mystic of the fifteenth-sixteenth centuries, cries: "My God is me." The mystic is the one who in the words of a modern visionary, the poet Jessica Powers enters "into the secret places / Filled with life."

However, such entry comes not to those caught up "where the air is rare," not to the faint-hearted or ivory-towered bound. Searching the chambers deep within requires a doggedness that comes only to someone who has lived life in its reality, grasped its rough edges and not let go because of the rub of them. Elizabeth Dreyer notes that the openness characteristic of the mystic is remarkably similar to what she lists as one quality of a "feminine mode of being," that of vulnerability. Such vulnerability, the product of free choice and lived experience, "can emerge only after one has developed a positive sense of control and responsibility about life."

Some of the most mystical of women I have encountered along the way are the most real. One was a young woman whom I treated for several years in therapy. Her history was a sadly familiar one of early sexual abuse, abandonment first by her natural mother, later by her adopted one. She came into treatment suffering the horrors of a body that was betraying her, presenting physical symptoms for which there was no physical source. At one time she described herself as a throwaway. But her favorite image was a torn rag. "I'm dirty and useless and full of holes." Toward the end of her sessions, the image changed; the rag became lace. "It's full of holes, too, but the holes make a pattern; they create beauty."

The most mystical encounter she shared followed her acceptance into a Society of Friends. "A fallen away atheist," for years she had searched for a faith stance in which she could find meaning. Finally, among this group of "true friends" who would listen to her confusion and still love her, she had found the tolerance, reservation of judgment and true care that she had lacked in family. One day she told me that she knew she had come home when she was able to rise among them and give testimony. In true Quaker tradition, she spoke of a sense of an "inner light" whose truth and force she felt come to life. "It was like giving birth," she shared. "I opened my mouth not even knowing what would come out and I spoke truth. I told of God's having found me and my having found God."

Another woman mystic I have been privileged to know was in one of my freshman psychology classes. "The grandmother of the group" as she called herself, she truly was such, having been the mother of five and now grandmother for a whole retinue of children. With her "empty nest" facing her, she had decided to return to school, to take the classes that interested her and "just grow and enjoy." What she added to the class of eager young women was a rich experience of life, hardwon and holy.

One day she told me before class of a walk in the woods she had taken the weekend before. While the autumn leaves lay thick on the ground and a thin veil of mist filled the air, she arrived in the course of her hike at a "spot of sunlight." She described how cradled in a few square inches of warmth, three small but brilliant violets poked their faces up. "I knew God was in that spot; it was truly holy ground." With these words she echoed for me the ancient mystics—Jacob building his altar at Bethel, Moses awed before the burning bush, Anna and Simeon holding the mystery child in the temple precincts. Like these great foreparents, my little lady was open to the moment, awake and aware and so able to catch the fragment of the divine inbreaking into the ever-so-ordinary. On a day marked in shadow and deep in dying, she uncovered life. This is the everyday mystic, the woman gifted with a sense of inner space.

This is the essence of the contemporary poet, contemplative and, yes, mystic—Jessica Powers. Robert Morneau in introducing her book of selected poetry uses Joseph Conrad's picture of the artist as her prologue: "...behold!—all the truth of life is there: a moment of vision, a sigh, a smile—and the return to an eternal rest." This woman, only recently recognized as the incredibly gifted poet that she is, has in over 400 poems captured the breath of a mystic in the very ordinary and commonplace. Like the violets hidden in the dying autumn leaves, she finds evidence of God, of "particular grace" in the most mundane and often overlooked, elements of joy in the course of great sorrow and grief.

Jessica Powers died just a few years ago, and had spent over forty years as a member of a Carmelite monastery. Before her entrance there her life was a mixture of scholarship and secretarial duties, rural farmland communities and high rise concrete as she moved between her native Wisconsin and periods spent in Chicago and New York. The years etched against the stark farm country earned her appellation as a "winter poet." Her lines are woven with images of frost and snow with "iridescent trees of ice" and "white foliage of upper air," the "coins of silver" she collects for herself and others. Yet, Jessica Powers' true home was neither the open countryside nor the busy city streets, but the place and space within. Morneau notes, "Between the lines of all her verse lies hidden the doctrine of the divine indwelling."

Strongly influenced by the probings of the poet of dark night, St. John of the Cross, she described her experience of mysticism in terms of "the house at rest." She in a true womanly sense of inner space sees herself, the searcher, as the "tenant" who at midnight is "free to take the kindled heart and go" deep within the "humble silences" and midnight silenced rooms. She describes a place that is the epitome of "potential emptiness." Prayer, she personifies as "the mystic entering in / to secret places filled with light."

But the poem that speaks most powerfully of Jessica Powers' achievement of inner space comes in one written a few years after her entrance into Carmel, "There is a Homelessness." Throughout the stanzas she demonstrates her mysticism of the ordinary, depicting the "homelessness" of the searching soul in terms of dining on bored crumbs, of unknown leaves from "unimaginable trees." In her final lines she makes the transition to the transfixed soul as she owns the pain of separation, "the pain of the mystic suddenly thrown / back from the noon of God to the night of his own humanity."

Jessica Powers would have loved and celebrated my two mystics, the struggling young woman who found "inner light" among the Friends and the grandmother who uncovered her "particular grace" one grey autumn day. She speaks for many modern women mystics searching to find their own inner space by becoming wholly feminine.

Chapter Two
A Woman Celebrates Bringing to Life

W hen Miriam steps out on the banks of the Red Sea and celebrates her moment of truth, she stands as most maternal in the sense of most fecund and fruitful. From her struggle within she gives birth to a word, a word that will become a unifying song for her people. Such is the gift of woman that is a bringing to birth, a creativity that encompasses the physical processes of conception, gestation and birthing, but that reaches far beyond these.

In a beautiful essay, "In Search of Our Mother's Gardens," that celebrates the struggle and survival of her people, especially the history of African-American women,

Alice Walker shares a very personal image; it is her own mother's garden. Scratched from the dry clay of a sharecropper's patch, in whatever house Walker's family lived, her mother's rare and wondrous array of flowers filled their front yard. "Not just your typical scraggly country stand of zinnias, either" but wild profusions of colors and exotic blooms. Walker wonders how and when her mother found time and energy to plant and dig and weed after days working in the field with her father and evenings spent cleaning, cooking, sewing for her children. The conclusion she reaches about her own mother and so many of the foremothers of her people is that without their various sources of creativity, these women would have died, if not in body then in mind and soul. The "saints and lunatics" of her heritage, as she calls these women, kept alive for her and future generations of women the gift of creativity and this kept them alive through years of hardship, dirtpoor poverty and often great physical cruelty and degradation, even at the hands of their own.

Walker speaks of her own mother and other mothers and grandmothers as creators in words reminiscent of the yahwehistic account of creation in Genesis 2, a redeeming of life from dark and chaos. This reminds me of another woman, a medieval mystic living in a century perhaps as troubled and threatening as that of Walker's ancestors, the anchorite Julian of Norwich. (The author Carol Lee Flinders provides helpful background on mystics.) Her famous echo, "All shall be well and all manner of things shall be truly well" sounds not as pollyanna naiveté but of the wisdom of a woman who looked at plague-ridden streets, the core of inner city evils, the anguish and suffering in her own heart and those of others and still fashioned with optimism, hope and endurance a place of sanctuary where indeed "all shall be well."

This is the maternal vision of God Christ that Julian delineates so well, a vision that looks past surface superficialities into the heart. It is a vision of God that not only creates in a fatherly sense, planting the seed and bringing into existence, but in the motherly sense of nurturance and care, acceptance and forgiveness that perdures throughout life. It is the feminine aspect of God that balances the God of the Old Testament, forging and fashioning, with the gentle touch of comfort and consolation brought by Jesus in his message of "Abba" and images of the good shepherd and the woman in search of the lost coin.

The image of gardens and mother-God recalls a New Testament garden motif and moment of encounter, one that occurs in John 20. The garden now is that used for the burial of Jesus, the time is "very early on Sunday morning, while still dark" (vs. 1), and the woman who arrives as searcher is Mary Magdalene, one who knew well the healing, forgiving, penetrating divine vision of Jesus, mother-God. She comes when night still grips the earth, time's night, but also a personal night with Jesus still locked in death to her, still lost. She waits in silence and sorrow but obviously hope and in this pregnancy knows life. Her openness is mirrored in the mouth of the empty tomb that announces promises fulfilled. Her silence is broken by the whisper of her name. To speak a name in scriptural understanding is to reach to the core of the person. "Mary," says the Lord. "Rabboni," she answers and they know each other in the fullest sense of the word. In her willingness to wait through the darkness, she gives birth to the Word, a word she carries as "disciple to the disciples," the first real annunciation of Christ risen.

In her reflections on the transposition of this garden scene with that of the Garden of Eden, Madonna Kolbenschlag notes that the evils entering the world with the fall of humankind are reversed with the coming of that Sabbath light and personified in the encounter of Mary Magdalene and Jesus that Easter. Life is reclaimed from death, pain is made the tool of joy and procreation, cursed for women as marked by pain and unfilled longing in Eden, is transformed into creativity, a bringing to life that is the call of all Christians. "I have come that you may have life, life to the full" (John 10:10).

This brings two key themes forward for women's reflections on their gift for bringing to life. One concerns the conflicting attitudes toward bodiliness and its connections with women and their spirituality. The other centers on maternity and the message it holds as women struggle to find the meaning of this call among other calls to life.

The curse of women that resounds from the moment of betrayal and fall (Gen 3:16) fills the pages of scripture and history with problematic perspectives. Much of the problem focuses on issues about the body, with the physical as the center of human concupiscence. In this view women bear much of the stigma, and the conjoint images of blood and water, so significant of feminine physicality, symbolize much of the controversy. Throughout both testaments references to woman's flow of blood, her reproductive organs and the very processes of procreation alternate between allusions to defilement (Lev 12:2-5, Ez 16:4-8), pain (John 16:21), the world of the dead (2 Esd 4:41), and the cause of death (Gen 35:16-20; Is 37:3) to joy (John 16:21), fulfillment (Is 66:7-90) and the very mystery of the incarnation (1 John 5:6) with some of the contradictory verses located in the same books. The medieval mystics, according to Flinders, reflected this same duality about the nature of the body human and especially the body woman. They moved from a repudiation of the body as the source of fallenness with the very processes of incarnating, "giving flesh" to the infant, seen as part of the denigration, to a transformative view of woman as the one who gave nourishment, provided milk and in a more generic sense fashioned the loaves and spread the table.

Many women still wrestle with the remnants of this biblical curse and its Neoplatonic aftermath as seen in evidences of self-mutilation, extremes of anorexia, bulimia and obesity symptomatic of psychological imbalances, and even in confusion of the place of the female body in modern society as witnessed in pornography, sexual harassment and violation, and on a less drastic but more pervasive scale in modern media depictions.

Yet, many theologians and spiritual writers celebrate a rediscovery of the sacredness of the body, especially for and among women. Elizabeth Dreyer calls this "one of the hallmarks of contemporary spirituality" and notes that women have been specially blessed in a return to a sense of bodiliness in our times and expressions of worship. The rhythms within the female body that keep the biological clock ticking also tie women into a communion with the immanent God. So we, like Miriam, enter into religious dance and gesture, liturgical rite and ritual, hours of prayer and meditative postures with a greater naturalness because of our sense of bodiliness.

In the newfound reverencing of the body as sacred comes a broadened sense of creativity, more of what Eric Erikson meant by generativity, a nurturing of life, a being responsible and wanting to leave the stamp of myself on some part of my world. No matter what path a woman's life takes she must give birth in some way, either physical or spiritual. To be woman is to bring to life; it is simple as that. To celebrate being woman is to bring to "life to the full." What this means for the single woman, the woman religious, the woman after she has raised a family, is very much the same as what it means for the woman who accepts the formation of a family through the birth of a child. It means knowing the joys and sorrows of some kind of conceiving, bringing into the world and creating a world in which those entrusted to us can grow responsibly and wholly. It means stepping forth with faith and trust into the unknown for all that the future holds.

It means making promises in the question marks of the present and believing that the days and years to come somehow consecrate fidelity to those promises.

How this is expressed is as different as the women who take on the challenge of creativity. With my own commitment to celibacy I have struggled to remain true to the feminine gift of bringing to life and hold fast to my singlehearted dedication to God and God's church and I have witnessed this struggle in the lives of fellow women religious. My own answer lies in one way in the pages before you. I give life through writing. As I moved to the final stages of this book, it struck me that I had begun the actual process in June only to finish by deadline in February, a stretch of nine months, more than a little symbolic. I recall once working on an extensive writing project that went before a committee, only to see it drastically changed and edited. The feeling, as I expressed it to a friend, was that of watching my own newborn's arms and legs being ripped off and refitted in other places. This is truly symbolic of bringing to life, watching growth and knowing the challenge of handing over control. Erikson says the ability to master such setting free is a major sign of maturing in creativity.

Others among the women with whom I have worked have given life in many forms: in adorning sacred places for liturgical celebrations, in chanting psalms and singing the blues, in baking cookies and spreading a feast, in throwing a party and listening to others with heartwon advice, warm wisdom or comforting silence. The work of ministry, whatever form it takes, can provide a means of creating. True, devotion to one's work can become a substitute for growth and escape from dealing with reality. Women who become workaholics to deny their fear of sterile emptiness or failed relationships, as well as those who use their ministries as sources of need fulfillment, are giving birth in barrenness and self-absorption. Many of them are propagating dependencies among others as a way of gratifying their need to serve rather than as a maturing to Christian service. In the same way I have seen young women commit to marriage and bring children into the world to find the family security they desperately lacked in their own development. Sadly, what they discover, as do many of these other women searching for fullness outside themselves, is that the empty deserts of loneliness and insecurity cannot be filled by another. They must first find the core of life within themselves and the truth that their "hearts will be restless" until they reconcile the gift of potential emptiness.

True fullness of Christian service comes not through need fulfillment but through *diakonia*. This vision of service derived from the spirit of the early apostolic community is one of testing the generosity of one's own gifts and talents against the limits of the community's needs and response. The history of women, both personally and culturally, has often been one of struggle in service to *diakonia*, when the faith community of which they are participants is unwilling or unable to accept the offerings they feel called by God to make. Such rejection of the gifts of their creativity leads to a spiritual barrenness, as well as disenfranchisement and powerlessness.

Several contemporary women writers, among them Monika Hellwig and Sandra Schneiders, have emphasized the mirror side of this disenfranchisement in that the heritage women have borne, in being excluded from roles of leadership, from ritualized ministry and from positions of power have led to creative responses on their part. Schneiders notes that these very exclusions have opened women to remain true to a ministry of pastoral service, have better prepared them to form nonhierarchical communities and have gifted them with an awareness of and ability to respond to the needs of the marginalized and poor. Hellwig adds that the lack of power that hierarchical structures have imposed on individual women over the centuries has often forced them to band together into sisterhoods to work for societal change and removal of oppression. So we have the communities forged by such women as Elizabeth Seton, Frances Cabrini, Dorothy Day and Mother Teresa of Calcutta as witness of bringing to life against the forces of death.

Part of the challenge of bringing to birth, seen in both the process of delivery itself as well as in the years that follow, comes in the ability of the mother to hold on and let go. Anyone who has seen a child born into the world knows the terror and ecstasy bound into the pushing and pulling that is the physical effort. Anyone who has watched a parent say goodbye to a kindergarten youngster that first day of school can empathize with the doublebind of wanting this little one off on his/her own and wishing for nothing so much as to hug the youngster closely and take him/her home to security and safety. Sara Ruddick in a very contemporary and insightful presentation on maternal cognition speaks of a metaphysical attitude that comes from generations of inculturation in women's holding on and letting go. The same mother who hugs her baby to her crooning lullabies at bedtime is the one who in the middle of the night insists that this little one can stay in the crib and bear the frights of the dark with the comfort of mommy's good night kiss and the small glow of a night light to reassure. This is the "good enough mother" of the object relation psychologists, theorists like David Winnicott, who insist on the criticality of the holding environment so intuitive in mothers, a place of balance between safety and independence, with the wise knowing what child needs which of these attitudes at a particular time.

Again the gifts of this maternal cognitive style are not solely those of mothers. I have watched high school teachers deal with similar struggles in their efforts to get soon-to-graduating seniors unattached from the umbilical cord of their hometown and into the new worlds of the college campus. In counselors with whom I have worked I have seen this delicate balance expressed in the gentle weaning from dependency that must take place for health to happen with their clients. I have witnessed it in the dilemmas of the "sandwich generation" who wrestle with their dual responsibilities to children and parents and who must learn how to give care without creating dependencies.

The lesson of the delicate balance between holding on and letting go became most clear in my life through the person of a young woman client whom I'll call Katie. Following the breakup of an abusive marriage, Katie had been in a serious car accident in which she was thrown through the windshield. Several plastic surgeries later, she was still terrified to drive and fearful about recurrence of "that kind of pain." Physically, emotionally and financially drained, she had returned to her parents' home but now "felt trapped, a little girl again, smothered by an overprotective mother." What brought her to seek help, however, was none of these problems, but her involvement in a relationship with a married man, the father of several pre-adolescent children. While admitting that he held no future for her and often angry at feeling used by him, she seemed unable to put into action the decisions that would set her free. As time went on in our work together, I came to a realization: she and I seemed stuck.

This stuckness caused me to look at my interactions and certain uncharacteristic responses that I was beginning to make with Katie. I found myself going very cautiously in our sessions, weighing my words very carefully and worrying about her between appointments—all signs that I should look at the dynamics between Katie and myself with my supervisor. He helped me to gain one insight by focusing on the other "fragile persons" of whom Katie reminded me, persons I was perhaps ministering to through her. They ranged from my younger sisters, one in particular who even resembled Katie physically, to high school and college girls I had worked with and taught, to even parts of my more vulnerable self. But the real breakthrough came through another avenue. My supervisor asked very gently, "And aren't you doing to Katie what all the other major people in her life do? Her 'ex' who still hangs around, her overprotective mother, even the man with whom she's presently involved. They shield her, make her decisions for her and prevent her from growing up, taking responsibility. You have to help her look at what in her is calling forth this in others. This is no coincidence." It made sense. I, like so many others, was turning Katie into a doll person, like Nora of Ibsen's famous play *A Doll's House*. We had all accepted this dependent, needy Katie and were supporting her in that role. When she and I came to look at her life through these lenses, we got unstuck and she began to make some progress toward self-determination, decisiveness, responsibility. Both she and I had reached into our gifts of creativity and brought life out of death.

The woman who stands for me as the model of bringing to life in every sense of that phrase is the gifted poet, essayist, dancer, Gospel singer and civil rights worker, Maya Angelou. While she is indeed a mother in the physical sense of the word, she seems to have achieved the status of maternity in all its definitions. Struggling out of an early history of abandonment, abuse and elective mutism, she has become a voice for the silenced of her people and all who celebrate life.

One of the most moving and telling scenes of her gift to both create and be created comes in the fifteenth chapter of her autobiography, *I Know Why the Caged Bird Sings*. The incident is a small one as far as history goes, but in her life it is critical, the point when one of her mother-figures, Mrs. Flowers, "threw me my first lifeline." Terrified into mutism by the murder of the man she accused of raping her on the streets of St. Louis, Maya was as a child locked in her own world. Able to read, to write, to study, she refused to speak and so had little ahead of her in a world where even the whole and healthy struggled to eke out an existence. What Mrs. Flowers gave her on a summer afternoon of tea, cookies, and homemade lemonade, was the gift of finding a creative core, an inner self alive and respondent. From this aristocratic woman from the wrong side of the railroad tracks Maya received both confrontation and compassion. With her gentle grace and warm smile she communicated a sense of personal worth and forgiveness to this victimized little girl. Through her demands that Maya use her gifts she opened up for this child and for the world the rich resources of the spoken and sung word, the deep richness of mother-wit, and the penetrating insights of a woman who would grow to stand beside princes and presidents, civil rights leaders and ghetto derelicts and to reach out with rare gifts of holding on and letting go.

What Angelou's story signifies, besides her own

embodiment of creativity, is that besides the parent-child interaction, so many relationships depend on the tenuous balance arranged between holding on and letting go. Whether in the delicate dance of intimacy between husband and wife, the communal bonds of a religious house, pastoral team or business community, the educative push-pull of teacher and student, counselor and client, the discernment of knowing when to move forward, when to withdraw, what times call for speaking, what times for silence and always with whom—all require the maternal cognition and intuition that Winnicott describes as the essence of the "good enough mother." While most relationships, like most children, have a certain resiliency capable of adjusting to lapses in the maintaining of such an environment, over the long haul consistency in providing the balance proves the formation ground of hearts and lives and souls. It is over the long haul that the "valiant women" of today, faced with so many threats to maintaining balance, draw upon their gifts of bringing to life.

Chapter Three
A Woman Celebrates Waiting

What sets Miriam apart from the Israelite people as they stand on the threshold of their exodus is her ability to seize the moment, to look at the here and now and to grasp the portent it holds. She is only able to do that because of her openness to its possibilities, an openness formed deep within her over time and nurtured into life. In this receptivity to the moment Miriam manifests the best of a woman's gift of waiting.

Saying "the best" suggests that there can be a "worst" in waiting and such is the case. Waiting has come to be a hallmark of the feminine role and it carries both positive and negative aspects for feminine development. In looking with honesty at waiting, at its gifts and costs, I am reminded of two women with whom I have been closely associated during a critical waiting time for each. Both, suffering for several months with serious illnesses, have been bound into enforced periods of waiting: for laboratory results, for medical decisions, for outcomes of studies, for consultations, for drug reactions. While both share similar life-threatening diagnoses and both are locked into a waiting time, each woman has faced her waiting in very different ways.

The first woman, a good friend whose wisdom I have long valued, has listened to the surgeons, asked for second opinions, weighed the various recommendations, sought advice and support among friends and family, read and researched, and worked to bring about the best healing possible. The other woman, long a concern to those who care about her, has sat often wrapped in the darkness of her room, silent and solitary. She hears the doctors, but doesn't listen, is often unsure of what they have said, can't remember their reports, doesn't act on their recommendations and turns away from those who come bearing hope, life, compassion. She seems to expect that healing, if it comes, will arrive from someone, someplace outside herself. Both women are waiters, in that they have no choice, but my friend is the personification of the active waiter. The other woman is a victim, the embodiment of passive waiting.

Much has been written and researched in recent years about waiting as a feminine mode of being with both its up and down sides. Waiting is a necessity of life; in a sense a great equalizer for it comes to all—rich and poor, old and young, men and women. Yet, waiting does seem to "play favorites" in that the poor, the old, and women seem much more often to be called to assume a waiting stance. For women to embrace waiting as gift in their lives, they need to come to an understanding of the vast difference between passive and active waiting as each is manifested both culturally and personally.

Waiting as defined by traditional society is seen as reaction rather than action, a type of existence that forces those in a waiting mode to be dependent on others for decisions, movement, direction. Culturally, we see the image of the questing knight setting off on his crusades while the lady of the castle serves by "standing and waiting his return." He quests, conquers, explores; she holds the fort. What such a waiting stance has imposed on women is a sense of powerlessness, lack of control, goal or direction about their lives. Standing by castle moats provides little in terms of discovering a world beyond your doorstep. And while castles and crusades have faded to pages of history books and fairy tales, the enclosed worlds of suburban neighborhoods, parochial concerns and narrow networks of relationships build walls as high as any moated fortress.

Part of the constriction that marks passive waiting comes from historical conditioning, but part comes from personal decision. The pervasiveness of conditioning can be seen in many of the archetypal figures of women over the ages. Look no further than the fairy tale heroines that little girls (and boys) go to sleep hearing. Stories of Cinderella, Snow White, Sleeping Beauty tell of passive waiters: women who sit, stand or lie, sometimes dormant, until their knight errant rides to the rescue. It was pointed out to me in a recent class discussion of such archetypal figures that more current heroines presented in animated films, characters like Belle of *Beauty and the Beast* fame or Jasmine of *Aladdin*, appear more assertive, decisive and active than was typical of heroines past.

What these fantasy figures of the past represent is a truth, at least as culturally held, of what women's experience was and was meant to be. It reflects the reality contained in the adage that traditional woman's work, measured from sunrise to sunset, was never done. When women's sole domain was the home, few tasks were marked with any sense of closure. The beds made today would be tomorrow's chore too; the meals prepared were soon eaten with the next to be started. Time was often set by the schedules of children. Feeding hours, bedtime rituals, midnight awakenings, the necessary focus on the constant, daily needs of a family set a new pace for time, a time over which the woman held little control. She became locked into a circular pattern very different from the linear direction of the world running along a historic, chronological flow.

As a result of this time-out-of-time experience, part

of women's cultural experience is obviously negative with consequent feelings of powerlessness, loss of control and direction often leading to a sense of diminished autonomy, effectiveness and even self-worth. However, several positive features are made more readily available to women if they open themselves to them. One is that their experience makes them, like Miriam, more ready to seize the moment, to live in the here and now and look for the possibilities that lie within today. A mother tuned into the breathing of her baby is the first to recognize any change from the usual. A woman in touch with the most subtle movements in those closest to her can sense before any words are spoken, communication in all its forms. Such receptivity is the herald to entering into the gentle movements of the Spirit within. Such waiting on the pulse of breath can open to the very breath of God.

Such, too, is the doorway to an experience of time that has been called by various writers mythic time, sacramental time, kairotic time, the genetic moment. Lifted out of the ordinary flow, of time measured in seconds and hours, of days marked by schedules, exciting things can happen. Minutes can stretch and hold great meaning for time to come. Whole worlds of wonder can open in a few seconds. A person can fall in love, witness one of nature's miracles, give birth, touch a life forever, die—all in the space of a blink or a breath. Many of us tap into this kairotic time even in the course of our ordinary lives. When I enter into a retreat and give myself over to the mystery of its own rhythms letting God set the agenda, I know the freedom of being lifted out of schedules, deadlines, and routine. Insights come; ideas flow; memories emerge; feelings are released. God speaks in such moments. Such is a gift that comes more easily to woman awake to the potential in today.

However, just as passive waiting has exerted a negative influence culturally on feminine formation, so too can it enter private and personal lives with devastating force. I have seen the hold such passivity has in the hunched bodies of some of the clients who have come locked in their defeat. I have seen it even more in their eyes, eyes that search the ground, that refuse to look up into another's face, eyes that mirror emptiness within. The first time I saw such eyes were actually in laboratory animals. Back in the 1970s when Martin Seligman was working with experiments on "learned helplessness," I watched spellbound as he demonstrated the inability of dogs to jump to escape shock. By submitting these laboratory animals to sequences of uncontrollable, inescapable pain, he had in his experimental cages created victims as real and tragic as any social drop-out, any street person, any despairing victim of "learned helplessness."

As I observed these cringing, whining dogs, I recalled a short story I had read once in a literature class. James Joyce, the self-imposed exile, poet and author of Ireland, wrote a series of short stories under the title of *Dubliners*, imaging his native land as caught in a paralysis, a sort of slow sinking to its death. In one narrative in this collection, the title character, a young woman named

Eveline is shown as trapped in her "dusty" Dublin home, locked in by family responsibilities, a misguided sense of duty, deathbed promises made to her mother long ago, but above all held captive by her fears—fear of change, of the new, of challenge, of growth, of love, of life. In the course of the few pages that tell the story we see Eveline fighting to decide—should she stay in the alcoholic, abusive home waiting for life to be different or should she seize the moment, grab hold of the possibility for change that lies before her in the person of the young sailor Frank and his marriage proposal that will mean a new life for her in Buenos Aires. The story closes tragically, with Eveline standing frozen, paralyzed, clinging to the guardrail while the ship and Frank sail far from her. Joyce describes her at that moment:

> "She set her white face to him, passive like a help-less animal. Her eyes gave no signs of love or farewell or recognition."

Like Eveline, like the solitary invalid of my opening, many women do become victims of learned helplessness because their personal histories have conditioned them to expect little from life, to accept pain as their lot, to look for no answers, no escape. Such is often the case with abused women, locked into violent relationships from which they see no exit. Such is the experience of the poor for whom waiting is a way of life, who must look to others for some rescue, some way out of bad neighborhoods, lack of education, limited resources, cramped housing.

The opposite of passivity is the stance of the active waiter. Personified in my friend who took on her illness almost as a challenge, it is marked by initiation, action, a sense of fidelity and promise and above all receptivity. This is the gift side of waiting at its best.

If passive waiting has its classic figures in feminine archetypes, so does active waiting. The mythical epitome who assumes such status is Penelope, the faithful wife of Ulysses, captured in the epic *Odyssey*. Bound to a mission of "standing and waiting" through the twenty-year absence of her hero husband, she transforms the time into a commitment to marriage fidelity through her creativity. Promising to marry a suitor chosen from the one hundred-plus prospects only when she finishes weaving her father-in-law's shroud, she delays the moment by unraveling her work at the end of each day. During the course of her two-decade wait for her husband, she manages her home, her family, her husband's property and the outcome of history through gentle wisdom and inventiveness.

Such is the challenge for contemporary women who assume the stance of the active waiters. They have been delineated with penetrating insight by Constance FitzGerald in a study of enforced waiting she terms "feminine impasse." Feminine impasse is an experience of being trapped in the dark with no light at the end of the tunnel to signal escape. In trying to find some release from a sense of social helplessness and disempowerment, logic, rationality and right-brained analysis fail. No ordinary solutions work. This condition, a universal one, seems compounded in a post-nuclear age given over to technology, "cold reason and deadly logic." The answer FitzGerald supplies is to turn to contemplation, to fall to our knees in a sense of accepted helplessness, to let go and let God. But the surrender she calls for is not the mute defeat of the victim of learned helplessness. She challenges women to hand over their very powerlessness to the inspiration and power of God. In the surrender comes the seizing of the moment, for she notes that it is only when all rational options fail that creative imagination enters in and all kinds of possibilities open up. When time, order and system shut down, the kairotic moment explodes and God steps into human time.

This passage through nothingness into the divine puts contemporary women into a frame of reference that internalizes for them the true option of the poor and disenfranchised of the world. With other marginalized persons they form a community of *anawim*, the faithful remnant of waiters and watchers who in biblical tradition preserved the possibility of salvation among the chosen people. Only by standing with the poor, speaking for and with them, does option for the poor become real and we say from the depth of experience no longer "the poor," but "we poor."

While I have never known the gnawing ache of going to bed without a meal or the bone-crunching pain of a winter night on the street, I have felt the fingers of poverty grip my heart. I, with other women religious of various communities, have looked into the future and wondered where in the dark lies any kind of light for regrowth, any hope for survival. I have heard the voices of the old grieve, as for a dying family, the lack of vocations, wondering with a mourning for this community to whom they devoted their lives, who will carry on the work of the apostolates, who will be left to give vitality. I have heard the longing of the young for life-giving opportunities, for a past when a sense of identity provided a support, a bonding. When I touch on these losses and fears, I can stand with a poor woman worried about her children, her chances, her choices and say "we poor." And I know as surely as anyone desperate for survival that hope and future can come only with new vision and dynamic efforts.

When I look among the faces of contemporary women for one to model such active waiting, one leaps out among the many. She is not only the writer who penned a treatise on active waiting, *attente*, but one who etched its reality in her life. She is the French philosopher and academic turned factory worker, Simone Weil. In her own life, she often ran to excess and her desperate need to drive and deprive herself, while the stuff of martyrs, is not a blueprint for healthy living, but in her holding fast to a belief in active waiting on the God who waits on us, she has no equal. In her beautiful exposition called *Waiting on God*, Weil portrays the image of the divine as the patient beggar who stands before the doorway of humankind ready to die of hunger rather than lose the moment of hearing the knock of the master. She sees God's creatures as called to an *attente* no less focused in which our every moment becomes "an emptying, not seeking anything, but ready to receive in naked truth."

If her words seem extreme, her life mirrored their intensity. Surrounded by the poverty of the French factory system and seeing no logical economic solution for its abuses, she seized her only option for impasse—direct action. She gave up her comfortable position as professor of philosophy and joined the assembly line. Side by side with the poor, she came to know the dehumanization of a machine-dominated society, the loss of personal dignity of those caught in an industrial system, and the humiliation of those "who do not count—in any situation, in anyone's eyes—and who will never count, no matter what happens."

Even admitting that she always had the security of a supportive family and financial security to fall back on, Weil came to see the despair and darkness of a world with no escape. Like the *anawim* of old, she came to know the only power possible in such a world, the unlimited trust in God. She came to speak of an inner authority whose root is to forgive and to enter into brokenness, to accept and share our weakness and strength with others. As with few others, Simone Weil grasped the cost and gift that belongs to those who embrace real waiting, *attente*.

Chapter Four

A Woman Celebrates Prophecy

When Miriam broke into the song of victory for her people, she entered into her prophetic moment. The God whose mystery had shone before the Israelites in sun-filled cloud and night fire, now moves among them, a charismatic force making them one. It is the music and message of this woman who calls the transcendent El Shaddai, the Almighty One, to be their Yahweh, their "I will be who I will be." With this Miriam epitomizes all the aspects of her womanliness and celebrates them in her gift of prophecy.

The classic prophets of Old Testament fame, while very different from each other in personality, purpose and point of view, shared certain key characteristics that mark them as one. Two of these speak strongly for the gift of prophecy that women can tap into as part of their movement to God. These are all-encompassing qualities that for the sake of consideration we can call concreteness and connectedness.

While certain other groups among the Israelites such as the priests and royalty could trace a line of descendence, no such family tree could be claimed for the prophets. These speakers of God's word were called from among the people, for the sake of the people, for a specific time and message. As such they were very much individuals rooted in the human community, in touch with the lives of the people they were called to serve.

Part of their rootedness derives from their origins. Their call came out of the *klesis*, the stuff of their lives, and it is in the midst of that stuff that they move to their mission: their call to change and conversion. Amos and Jeremiah are sent forth from the isolated security of their rural villages to question the moral fiber of a whole nation. Isaiah, family man and father, must step from anonymity to challenge the political and religious powers of his age.

Their words, too, testify to their very human roots. Their vision falls so often on the commonplace, objects from their very human backgrounds: such images as almond trees in spring (Jer 1:11), a basket of summer

fruit (Amos 8:1), potter's clay (Jer 18:1-6), stumps and stones (Is 6:13; 28:16). Yet, in these simple features God is present as in the lives of their hearers. The difference is that the prophets look with divine vision, a peering, searing insight that can penetrate the barrenness and recognize in it potential for life.

A probing to the bone—such is the feminine insight that in its grounding in the very marrow of humanity finds access to mystical heights. This is often the pathway that feminine spirituality takes. A woman, whether influenced by nature or nurture, makes her leap to God and relationship with God often through the concrete and real. Argued at times as too restrictive of women's experience, there is gift in grounding. When tied to others, to human worries and wants, heartaches and happiness through the persons she loves, a woman is less likely to lose the face of her God in unreal abstractions. Forced through her experience of worship to see God as other, she knows God in the faces of others, not masses of humanity, but the lonely old couple in the apartment below, the single mother needing a lift home, the confused child hurt and alone.

When Mother Teresa of Calcutta first took up her ministry on the teeming streets of the Indian city, she was overwhelmed with the sea of misery that stretched before her. Each day multitudes lay in the gutters, dying of want and neglect. Her first impulse was a sense of drowning in the numbers and with it fear that she could never do enough. However, through the grace she found in her woman's heart, she was called to the side of one pathetic man. In the last few hours of his life, she brought him ease from pain, companionship in his agony; she brought him God. And from that experience, she formed her mission to the poor. She could not take on the thousands of poor in India, not even those on the Calcutta streets, but she could heal, whole and make holy—one by one by one.

When poverty takes on the face of a poor person, when wounded humanity cries in the eyes of one hurt child, the call comes from among the people to minister to the people. This is the spirituality of prophetic response: to allow the power of God within each person to reach inside each of us. This is part of the prophetic gift available to woman.

The other, the aspect of connectedness, is very much related to woman's being in tune with the concrete. The prophets of Israel could speak of God, through God, for God, only because they spoke to God. Each one, in wind and fire, in burning bush or violent sea, beside gourd plants or temple braziers, stood face-to-face with Yahweh. Because of their intimate experience of being God's friend, trustmate, confidant, they could call the people they were sent to serve to a like intimacy, to a community of presence, to a radical change of heart.

Very often it was through the owning of their personal faults, limits and woundedness that the prophet came to know God and God's goodness. In the course of the last decade, researchers into women's development have underscored that females develop best in the context of mutuality. Within a "web of relationships" women mature toward autonomy and self-direction. As anyone who has ever entered into relationship can testify, it is a testing ground for one's own human faults and foibles. Real maturity does not mean achieving an absence of faults and failures but an ability to see, to honor and to work to heal the human weaknesses. Only when I can reverence the wounds within myself can I call to accountability the community for whom my prophetic voice awaits.

Madeleine L'Engle has written a penetratingly poetic allegory of human life and love, often mistakenly catalogued as a children's classic called A *Wrinkle in Time.* In it three children undertake an epic journey through constellations and galaxies to rescue their missing father and to ultimately save the world. To support the children in their mission, three mythical creatures bestow the archetypal magical gifts on them. To Meg, humble and homespun, they donate "her faults."

"My faults . . . but I'm always trying to get rid of my faults." She comes to learn as Mrs. Whatsit predicts that it is in the owning of her limits that real strength is found. Meg saves herself, her father, brother, family, the entire course of human history, not through domination, arrogance or power, but through the sense of her littleness, her constant curiosity and a certain stubborn spirit.

Contemporary women are surrounded by forces of destruction as catastrophic as any galactic might faced by Meg. Sometimes the forces lie within the quiet neighborhoods of their own backyards in which apathy, stereotyping, exclusivity, superficiality and soap-opera addiction can kill with as much thoroughness as any radioactive material. Israel's prophets saw the insidious evil in such complacency: "You people hate anyone who challenges injustice and speaks the whole truth," cried the prophet Amos (5:10) and castigated them for thinking "that keeping quiet in times of evil is the smart thing to do" (5:13). The prophetic response of the times was to draw on strengths that women today can lay claim to: the ability to take on evil one by one by one and to address it out of the base of community.

Both of these become evident in women's efforts to "make peace, not war." Knowing that the contents of a body bag coming home from Somalia or Iran is the boy who once played ball down the street, translating body counts into fathers of families, sons and lovers, women can't think in terms of strategic victories or lines in the sand. Having tapped into the hurt of being the victim, the underdog, the have-not too often in history, they can't support efforts to perpetuate such philosophies. As Monika Hellwig notes, women can draw on their "usable pasts" to motivate themselves to work toward peace with such impetus coming from not vindication, but "from compassionate horror of the pain and suffering and bereavement that war causes, often to those who have least stake in its outcome."

Many women stand in the forefront these days as spokespersons of peace and workers for justice. Yet, it is not to any of these I look as the model of prophecy. The woman I choose as focus for these gifts is one who herself recognized her call to enunciate a "prophetic vision" as "a most terrible vocation." From the narrow confines of her rural Georgia farm where sickness and commitment to her Southern Gothic tradition held her, Flannery O'Connor reached out into a world she saw as locked in a deadly moral morass, blinded by a lack of awareness of personal salvation. "To the hard of hearing you shout," she said explaining the grotesque in her work, "for the almost-blind you draw large and startling letters." Her novels and short stories are graphic and gripping portraits of persons standing on the fringe of redemption with potential grace before their very hands. They only have to reach.

Like the classic prophets, O'Connor drew on the commonplace, the concrete, the very real—sometimes too real, as she sketched in the broken bodies and crippled souls of her characters the moral woundedness of her times. Her message to an audience who had lost a sense of God was to reach without and within. Without, grace lay all around, like air to a dying person, but most individuals walk around not even knowing they're breathing. Within lay Christ, the center of all possibility. With the hurt and hurting women of all ages, she would say that only in knowing the fall can you know the glory, only in enduring the passion does Easter become possible; only in knowing you are not God, do you come close to being so.

One of the most prophetic women I have encountered in my work lived and struggled in a world not much less grotesque than the ones drawn in large letters in O'Connor's stories. For over twenty years as wife and mother she had endeavored to love, support and bring to healing her husband, a man whose mood swings ranged from violent manic heights to death-wish depressions. By the time I came to know Julie the worst was over and medication had evened out somewhat the vast extremes of Bill's emotional life. But she spoke of the bad days when he said and did things that left her feeling broken and lost. "I would pray then for all the emptiness I felt. I would say over and over, like a mantra, 'Heart of Jesus, fill the heart of Julie. Heart of Jesus, fill the heart of Bill. Heart of Jesus, fill the space in between.'"

Fill the space in between—this is the place where the prophet stands calling God's people to a new vision of love and compassion. This is the place where God and person meet in the prophetic moment. This, too, is a woman's place.

Conclusion
A Woman Celebrates Paradox

As I read back over the pages of reflection on a woman's celebration of her movement to God, I see two threads weaving throughout the many words. One is a thread I would call "all of a piece." While I have spoken individually about the various themes, about a woman's call to interiority, creativity, waiting and prophecy, in a sense they are all part of the whole and can't be separated from each other. And that ultimately speaks truth, for each of these gifts celebrates life, some aspect of life that calls a woman into spiritual presence. From interiority comes the fertile ground

for the planting of the seed, the element of life. In the still quiet of active waiting the word comes to a fullness. In the birthing and bringing to life comes the possibility for nurturance and support. In the enforced waiting that expectation, growth and coming to fullness necessitate, a woman stands poised at the present moment, with time and all its nuances readying herself to be open. All comes together into a whole, intricate and integrated. All is "of a piece."

In the essay on her mother's garden that is Alice Walker's tribute to the women of her race, she shares another evocative image. She recalls the simple, yet exquisitely artistic, quilt that hangs in the Smithsonian Institute crafted by "an anonymous Black woman of Alabama, a hundred years ago." Pieced from rags and throwaway cloths, it depicts in crude and stark figures the moment of the crucifixion. I think often of that unknown, unnamed woman, probably a slave who gathered through her days the relics of material no one else wanted or needed. Perhaps in the beginning she had no thought of making this quilt; no concept of what form its design would take; she certainly never imagined the place it would one day hold in history. She just took the stuff of her days and wove a life—hers and God's.

This is what I tried to do in the bits and pieces, the ideas and memories, the stories and selections of literature that speak to me of celebrating the woman I am. I took the stuff of my days as shared with others and wove a life—a woman's in love with a God she was each day discovering. In this I feel very much in communion with so many women from my past and from the past I celebrate. So many, out of the stuff of their days, the quiet moments and upheavals, the experiences of hurt and healing, have fashioned a life. Often the finished product assumed a vastly different shape from the dream they held as young brides, hopeful novices or ambitious college students, but often in the very difference lay their greatest challenge, forging influences and offerings of grace.

The other thread that seems to pervade the pages just completed is that of paradox. From the first chapter to the last story, contradictions join into a unity. Outside and inside, mystic and realist, divine to ordinary, death out of life, loss from gift, concrete to transcendent—all of these summarize the many impressions of a woman's celebration of her God. This, too, makes eminent sense as I reflect on it. A woman holds within her core the potential for all life and in that life carries the kernel of death. From first breath we move to our dying into God, and woman in her bodiliness and her spirituality celebrates this. "Today, I set before you life and death," the Lord challenges through the prophet Moses, "Choose life" (Deut 30:19). The final paradox lies in these lines. To choose life is to choose death—and woman knows this in the very heart of her being. That is why she can celebrate.

Finally, as I conclude these pages there are so many other stories, other women, other encounters that I want to include. I also think of other perspectives still to consider, but that too is part of life. We are told that Julian of Norwich, England's great writer and mystic, wrote only one book in her entire life, but she wrote it twice. The first time she recorded the content of her "shewings" immediately after their happening. The second she penned some twenty-five years later, virtually the same book, telling of the same visions, this time after a life lived trying to make meaning of their message.

In his book on the prophets, Elie Wiesel, that contemporary seer and survivor of the holocaust, speaks of another paradox—one of creation that holds for women a mystery that is the essence of their life. He says, "According to Jewish tradition, creation did not end with man (and woman), it began with them. When God created man (and woman), God gave them a secret—and that secret was not how to begin but how to begin again" (the inclusive language is mine). With Julian of Norwich, with Wiesel, with all who look into the heart of life, my hope is that in some of these words all who search for God may find some truth that helps them to "begin again."

Bibliography

Angelou, Maya. (1971). *I Know Why the Caged Bird Sings*. New York: Bantam Books.

Dreyer, Elizabeth. (1984). "Recovery of the feminine in spirituality." *New Catholic World*, March-April, 68-72.

FitzGerald, Constance. (1986). "Impasse and dark night." In Joann Wolski Conn (Ed.), *Woman's Spirituality: Resources for Christian Development*. New York: Paulist Press.

Flinders, Carol Lee. (1993). *Enduring Grace*. San Francisco: Harper.

Gallico, Paul. (1941). *The Snow Goose*. New York: Alfred A. Knopf.

Hellwig, Monika. (1985). *Christian Women in a Troubled World*. Mahwah, NJ: Paulist Press.

Joyce, James. (1954). "Eveline." In *Dubliners*. New York: The Modern Press.

Kolbenschlag, Madonna. (1986). *Women's Spirituality: Finding Our True Home*. Credence Cassettes.

Kansas City, MO: National Catholic Reporter Publishing.

L'Engle, Madeleine. (1962). *A Wrinkle in Time*. New York: Farrar, Straus and Giroux.

Merton, Thomas. (1961). *New Seeds of Contemplation*. New York: New Directions.

Ruddick, Sara. (1989). *Maternal Thinking: Toward a Politics of Peace*. New York: Ballantine.

Schneiders, Sandra. (1983). "The effects of women's experience on their spirituality." *Spirituality Today*, Summer, 35:2, 100-116.

Siegfried, Regina & Morneau, Robert (Eds.) (1989). *Selected Poetry of Jessica Powers*. Kansas City, MO: Sheed and Ward.

Walker, Alice. (1983). "In search of our mothers' gardens." *Womanist Prose*. San Diego, CA: Harcourt, Brace, Jovanovich.

Weil, Simone. (1959). *Waiting on God*. London: Fontana Books.

Wiesel, Elie. (1976). *Messengers of God*. New York: Random House.

ILLUMINATIONBOOKS

Other Books in the Series

Lessons from the Monastery That Touch Your Life
by M. Basil Pennington, O.C.S.O.

Little Pieces of Light...Darkness and Personal Growth
by Joyce Rupp

Spirituality, Stress & You
by Thomas E. Rodgerson

As You and the Abused Person Journey Together
by Sharon E. Cheston

Why Are You Worrying?
by Joseph W. Ciarrocchi

Joy, The Dancing Spirit of Love Surrounding You
by Beverly Elaine Eanes

Every Decision You Make Is a Spiritual One
by Anthony J. De Conciliis with John F. Kinsella